Extreme Living

Dawn McMillan

Contents

Extreme Places	2
Deserts	8
Tropical Rainforests	12
The Arctic	16
Antarctica	20
Glossary	24

Extreme Places

Some places on Earth are very hot, and some are very cold. Some places have a lot of water and plants. Others have very little water and not many plants.

a desert

a tropical rainforest

Antarctica

These places are **extreme**. Extreme places can be very hot, very dry, very cold or very wet!

Life in extreme places can be hard. But many animals and people have ways that help them live there.

Chameleons can live in hot deserts or wet rainforests.

Animals can live in extreme places. If they live in a cold place, they have thick fur to keep them warm.

This hare has thick fur to live in the Arctic.

This Arctic fox also has thick fur to keep warm.

People can live in extreme places. In hot places, they live in houses that stay cool.

This mud house keeps people that live in this desert cool.

Deserts

Deserts are very dry places. Some deserts are very hot. Not many plants can grow in deserts, so there is not much food.

Hot Deserts of the World

Camels

Camels live in the desert. They can go a long time without drinking water. Camels have a hump that holds fat. They can live off the fat in their humps.

Camels have long eyelashes, to keep the sand out of their eyes.

People of the Desert

People who live in the desert wear long, loose clothes. These clothes help them stay cool and **protect** them from the sun.

Desert people often move from place to place, to find food and water.

People who move from place to place to find food and water are called nomads.

Tropical Rainforests

Tropical rainforests are very hot and very wet. There are lots of tall trees.

Tropical Rainforests of the World

More different kinds of animals live in tropical rainforests than in any other places on Earth.

Jaguars

Jaguars can live in tropical rainforests. The colours in their coats **blend** with the colours of the forest.

Jaguars are good climbers. They hide in trees and jump onto their prey.

Jaguars are good swimmers, too. They catch fish in the river.

Tropical Rainforest People

People who live in tropical rainforests are often good at climbing trees to find food. They eat fruit, small animals and even insects. They are also good at fishing.

Some people in tropical rainforests don't wear many clothes. They don't need to! The weather is hot, and the trees protect them from the sun.

The Arctic

The Arctic is covered in ice and snow. It is a very cold place.

Polar Bears

Polar bears live in the Arctic. They have a thick layer of fat to keep them warm. They also have a thick coat of fur.

Female polar bears make dens in the snow to protect their **cubs** from the cold.

People of the Arctic

Many people live in the icy Arctic. They wear clothes made from animal fur to keep them warm.

These clothes are made from seal skins and fox fur.

Some people in the Arctic build houses out of snow. These houses are called **igloos**. Igloos look cold, but they can get very warm inside!

Igloos are made from blocks of ice. The ice blocks are packed together in a circle shape.

Antarctica

Antarctica is the coldest place on Earth. Not many animals live in Antarctica, and not many plants can grow there.

Antarctica is a desert! It hardly ever rains there.

Emperor Penguins

Emperor penguins live in Antarctica. They have a thick fatty layer of skin. This keeps them warm while they are swimming in the icy water.

On land, Emperor penguins **huddle** together to keep warm.

People in Antarctica

Some people go to Antarctica to work, but no one lives there all the time. People have to bring all their food to Antarctica when they stay there. They need to wear very warm clothes!

People working in Antarctica stay in huts like these.

Glossary

blend
to look like the environment; to camouflage

cubs
the name given to baby bears, such as baby polar bears

extreme
far from ordinary or normal

huddle
to crowd together

igloos
buildings made of blocks of snow and ice

protect
to keep safe